Tom Müller

Leaves of Grass

Walt Whitman's

LEAVES OF GRASS

Selected Poetry and Prose

Edited by C. Merton Babcock

Illustrated by Jim Spanfeller

HALLMARK EDITIONS

CONTENTS

'THE UNITED STATES THEMSELVES'
by C. Merton Babcock

Walt Whitman was born on a Long Island farm, May 31, 1819. He spent his early years attending school in Brooklyn. A virile and robust lad, he had an affinity for both city and country life. While he loved to romp on the beaches and feel the ocean-spray in his face, he also enjoyed mingling with the teeming masses in the "fascinating chaos" of the city. As a young man, he occupied himself as office boy, printer's devil, journeyman printer and country schoolmaster. At 19, he became editor of a Long Island newspaper, beginning a career in journalism which lasted for more than a decade. In 1847-48, working his way as a carpenter and builder, he made an extensive tour of the United States and Canada.

About this time, Whitman conceived the idea of writing a book of verses which would interpret the "American dream" as he had come to understand it. "The United States themselves," he decided, "are essentially the greatest poem," and he set about experimenting with a new verse form which he believed would represent democratic ideals better than traditional patterns of poetry. He developed a rhythmical chant which allowed him utmost freedom of expression and which seemed to expand before its subject like the American landscape itself.

In 1855, the poet brought out the first edition of *Leaves of Grass*—a much-praised 94-page volume which he spent the rest of his life revising and enlarging. The final edition, published in 1892, was the sixth revision of his work. All of the poems that follow are taken from this final edition, and the prose selections from his several other books.

Whitman found form for his thoughts in the objects of nature. "A morning-glory at my window," he said, "satisfies me more than the metaphysics of books." To represent democracy, he selected a simple and unimposing leaf of grass, "sprouting in broad zones and narrow zones," "growing among black folks as among white." While the poems, in one sense, advocate a doctrine of individualism, reflected in such lines as "I celebrate myself, and sing myself," they also promote ideas of companionship and of brotherhood. In one breath, the poet could say, "I wear my hat as I please indoors and out," and, in another, "I will accept nothing which all cannot have on the same terms." He had discovered the principle of unity or oneness which reconciles such apparent opposites as self and others, body and soul, war and peace, life and death.

As Whitman grew older, he assumed the appearance of a prophet or seer with a long, shaggy beard and piercing eyes. He devoted himself more and more to humanitarian causes, and, during the Civil War years, he spent some time in Washington, D.C., and in Virginia, visiting army hospitals as a volunteer nurse, while he supported himself with part-time work in the Army Paymaster's Office.

During this period, he acquired an intense admiration for Abraham Lincoln, whom he recognized as "the grandest figure yet on all the crowded canvas of the Nineteenth Century." The tragedies of war and Lincoln's death inspired some of Whitman's most unforgettable poems, including "O Captain! My Captain!" and "When Lilacs Last in the Dooryard Bloom'd"—one of the most beautiful elegies in the English language.

After working briefly in the Bureau of Indian Affairs, the poet, in 1873, suffered a partial paralysis which made him an invalid at his brother's home in Camden, New Jersey. Despite his condition, he was able, in 1879, to make another tour of the West. It allowed him to see again the country he loved.

Walt Whitman died in 1892, having bequeathed to the American people one of their most memorable books—full of good cheer, of hope and comradeship. In *Leaves of Grass*, crowded as it is with impressions, with the emotions of a maturing nation and the sensations of a burgeoning continent, we may truly rediscover America.

DEDICATION

Thou reader throbbest life
and pride and love the same as I,
Therefore for thee
the following chants.

Walt Whitman

INSCRIPTIONS

One's-Self I Sing

One's-Self I sing, a simple separate person,
Yet utter the word Democratic, the word En-Masse.

Of physiology from top to toe I sing,
Not physiognomy alone nor brain alone is worthy for
    the Muse, I say the Form complete is worthier far,
The Female equally with the Male I sing.

Of Life immense in passion, pulse, and power,
Cheerful, for freest action form'd under the laws divine,
The Modern Man I sing.

What Am I After All

What am I after all but a child, pleas'd with the sound
    of my own name? repeating it over and over;
I stand apart to hear—it never tires me.

To you your name also;
Did you think there was nothing but two or three
    pronunciations in the sound of your name?

The Prairie States

A newer garden of creation, no primal solitude,
Dense, joyous, modern, populous millions, cities and farm
With iron interlaced, composite, tied, many in one,
By all the world contributed—freedom's and law's and
                                        thrift's society,
The crown and teeming paradise, so far,
                              of time's accumulations,
To justify the past.

Song of Myself

I celebrate myself, and sing myself,
And what I assume you shall assume,
For every atom belonging to me as good belongs to you.
I loaf and invite my soul,
I lean and loaf at my ease observing a spear
                              of summer grass. . . .
A child said What is the grass? fetching it to me
                              with full hands;
How could I answer the child? I do not know what it is
                              any more than he.
I guess it must be the flag of my disposition,
                    out of hopeful green stuff woven.
Or I guess it is the handkerchief of the Lord,
A scented gift and remembrancer designedly dropt,

Bearing the owner's name someway in the corners,
       that we may see and remark, and say Whose?

Or I guess the grass is itself a child, the produced babe
       of the vegetation.
Or I guess it is a uniform hieroglyphic,
And it means, Sprouting alike in broad zones and
       narrow zones,
Growing among black folks as among white,
Kanuck, Tuckahoe, Congressman, Cuff, I give them
       the same, I receive them the same. . . .

In all people I see myself, none more and not one a
       barley-corn less,
And the good or bad I say of myself I say of them. . . .

I exist as I am, that is enough,
If no other in the world be aware I sit content,
And if each and all be aware I sit content. . . .
I dote on myself, there is that lot of me all so luscious,
Each moment and whatever happens thrills me with joy,
I cannot tell how my ankles bend, nor whence the
       cause of the friendship I take again.

That I walk up my stoop, I pause to consider
       if it really be,
A morning-glory at my window satisfies me more
       than the metaphysics of books. . . .

I believe a leaf of grass is no less than the journey-
                work of the stars,
And the pismire is equally perfect, and a grain of
                sand, and the egg of the wren,
And the tree-toad is a chef-d'oeuvre for the highest,
And the running blackberry would adorn the parlors
                of heaven,
And the narrowest hinge in my hand puts to scorn
                all machinery,
And the cow crunching with depress'd head
                surpasses any statue,
And a mouse is miracle enough to stagger sextillions
                of infidels. . . .

I have said that the soul is not more than the body,
And I have said that the body is not more than the soul,
And nothing, not God, is greater to one than one's
                self is,
And whoever walks a furlong without sympathy
                walks to his own funeral drest in his shroud,
And I or you pocketless of a dime may purchase the
                pick of the earth,
And to glance with an eye or show a bean in its pod
                confounds the learning of all times,
And there is no trade or employment but the young
                man following it may become a hero,
And there is no object so soft but it makes a hub for the
                wheel'd universe,

And I say to any man or woman, Let your soul stand
            cool and composed before a million universes.

And I say to mankind, Be not curious about God,
For I who am curious about each am not curious
                                    about God,
(No array of terms can say how much I am at peace
                        about God and about death.)
I hear and behold God in every object, yet understand
                            God not in the least,
Nor do I understand who there can be more wonderful
                            than myself.
Why should I wish to see God better than this day?
I see something of God each hour of the twenty-four,
                    and each moment then,
In the faces of men and women I see God, and in my
                        own face in the glass,
I find letters from God dropt in the street, and every
                    one is sign'd by God's name,
And I leave them where they are, for I know that
                        wheresoe'er I go,
Others will punctually come for ever and ever.

From Far Dakota's Cañons

From far Dakota's cañons,
Lands of the wild ravine, the dusky Sioux, the
                     lonesome stretch, the silence,
Haply to-day a mournful wail, haply a trumpet-note
                                 for heroes.

The battle-bulletin,
The Indian ambuscade, the craft, the fatal environment,
The cavalry companies fighting to the last in sternest
                                 heroism,
In the midst of their little circle, with their slaughter'd
                          horses for breastworks,
The fall of Custer and all his officers and men.

Continues yet the old, old legend of our race,
The loftiest of life upheld by death,
The ancient banner perfectly maintain'd,
O lesson opportune, O how I welcome thee!

As sitting in dark days,
Lone, sulky, through the time's thick murk looking in
                         vain for light, for hope,
From unsuspected parts a fierce and momentary proof,
(The sun there at the centre though conceal'd,
Electric life forever at the centre,)
Breaks forth a lightning flash.

Thou of the tawny flowing hair in battle,
I erewhile saw, with erect head, pressing ever in front,
                    bearing a bright sword in thy hand,
Now ending well in death the splendid fever of thy deeds,
(I bring no dirge for it or thee, I bring a glad
                                    triumphal sonnet,)
Desperate and glorious, aye in defeat most desperate,
                                    most glorious,
After thy many battles in which never yielding up a
                                    gun or a color,
Leaving behind thee a memory sweet to soldiers,   .
Thou yieldest up thyself.

I Hear America Singing

I hear America singing, the varied carols I hear,
Those of mechanics, each one singing his as it should
                                    be blithe and strong,
The carpenter singing his as he measures his plank
                                    or beam,
The mason singing his as he makes ready for work, or
                                    leaves off work,
The boatman singing what belongs to him in his boat,
                the deck-hand singing on the steamboat deck,
The shoemaker singing as he sits on his bench,
                    the hatter singing as he stands,

The wood-cutter's song, the ploughboy's on his way in
     the morning, or at noon intermission or at sundown,
The delicious singing of the mother, or of the young
              wife at work, or of the girl sewing or washing,
Each singing what belongs to him or her and to none else,
The day what belongs to the day—at night the party
              of young fellows, robust, friendly,
Singing with open mouths their strong melodious songs.

Once I Pass'd Through a Populous City

Once I pass'd through a populous city imprinting my
     brain for future use with its shows, architecture,
                              customs, traditions,
Yet now of all that city I remember only a woman I
     casually met there who detain'd me for love of me,
Day by day and night by night we were together—all
              else has long been forgotten by me,
I remember I say only that woman who passionately
                              clung to me,
Again we wander, we love, we separate again,
Again she holds me by the hand, I must not go,
I see her close beside me with silent lips sad and
                              tremulous.

DRUM-TAPS

Beat! Beat! Drums!

Beat! beat! drums!—blow! bugles! blow!
Through the windows—through doors—burst like a
                    ruthless force,
Into the solemn church, and scatter the congregation,
Into the school where the scholar is studying;
Leave not the bridegroom quiet—no happiness must
                    he have now with his bride,
Nor the peaceful farmer any peace, ploughing his field
                    or gathering his grain,
So fierce you whirr and pound you drums—so shrill
                    you bugles blow.

Beat! beat! drums!—blow! bugles! blow!
Over the traffic of cities—over the rumble of wheels
                    in the streets;
Are beds prepared for sleepers at night in the houses?
                    no sleepers must sleep in those beds,
No bargainers' bargains by day—no brokers or
                    speculators—would they continue?
Would the talkers be talking? would the singer
                    attempt to sing?

Would the lawyer rise in the court to state his case
                                    before the judge?
Then rattle quicker, heavier drums—you bugles
                                    wilder blow.

Beat! beat! drums!—blow! bugles! blow!
Make no parley—stop for no expostulation,
Mind not the timid—mind not the weeper or prayer,
Mind not the old man beseeching the young man,
Let not the child's voice be heard, nor the mother's
                                    entreaties,
Make even the trestles to shake the dead where they
                                    lie awaiting the hearses,
So strong you thump O terrible drums—so loud you
                                    bugles blow.

Year That Trembled and Reel'd Beneath Me

Year that trembled and reel'd beneath me!
Your summer wind was warm enough, yet the air I
                                    breathed froze me,
A thick gloom fell through the sunshine and darken'd me,
Must I change my triumphant songs? said I to myself,
Must I indeed learn to chant the cold dirges of the baffled?
And sullen hymns of defeat?

Race of Veterans

Race of veterans—race of victors!
Race of the soil, ready for conflict—race of the
conquering march!
(No more credulity's race, abiding-temper'd race,)
Race henceforth owning no law but the law of itself,
Race of passion and the storm.

How Solemn as One by One
(Washington City, 1865)

How solemn as one by one,
As the ranks returning worn and sweaty, as the men
file by where I stand,
As the faces the masks appear, as I glance at the faces
studying the masks,
(As I glance upward out of this page studying you,
dear friend, whoever you are,)
How solemn the thought of my whispering soul to
each in the ranks, and to you,
I see behind each mask that wonder a kindred soul,
O the bullet could never kill what you really are, dear
friend,
Nor the bayonet stab what you really are;

The soul! yourself I see, great as any, good as the best,
Waiting secure and content, which the bullet could
never kill,
Nor the bayonet stab O friend.

Adieu to a Soldier

Adieu O soldier,
You of the rude campaigning, (which we shared,)
The rapid march, the life of the camp,
The hot contention of opposing fronts, the long manoeuvre,
Red battles with their slaughter, the stimulus, the
strong terrific game,
Spell of all brave and manly hearts, the trains of time
through you and like of you all fill'd,
With war and war's expression.

Adieu dear comrade,
Your mission is fulfill'd—but I, more warlike,
Myself and this contentious soul of mine,
Still on our own campaigning bound,
Through untried roads with ambushes opponents lined,
Through many a sharp defeat and many a crisis, often
baffled,
Here marching, ever marching on, a war fight out—
aye here,
To fiercer, weightier battles give expression.

FROM DAWN TO STARRY NIGHT

Miracles

Why, who makes much of a miracle?
As to me I know of nothing else but miracles,
Whether I walk the streets of Manhattan,
Or dart my sight over the roofs of houses toward the sky,
Or wade with naked feet along the beach just in the
                            edge of the water,
Or stand under trees in the woods,
Or talk by day with any one I love, or sleep in the bed
                          at night with any one I love,
Or sit at table at dinner with the rest,
Or look at strangers opposite me riding in the car,
Or watch honey-bees busy around the hive of a
                          summer forenoon,
Or animals feeding in the fields,
Or birds, or the wonderfulness of insects in the air,
Or the wonderfulness of the sundown, or of stars
                        shining so quiet and bright,
Or the exquisite delicate thin curve of the new moon in
                        spring;
These with the rest, one and all, are to me miracles,
The whole referring, yet each distinct and in its place.
To me every hour of the light and dark is a miracle,

Every cubic inch of space is a miracle,
Every square yard of the surface of the earth is spread
                              with the same,
Every foot of the interior swarms with the same.
To me the sea is a continual miracle,
The fishes that swim—the rocks—the motion of the
                     waves—the ships with men in them,
What stranger miracles are there?

To the Sun-Set Breeze

Ah, whispering, something again, unseen,
Where late this heated day thou enterest at my
                                 window, door,
Thou, laving, tempering all, cool-freshing, gently
                                   vitalizing
Me, old, alone, sick, weak-down, melted-worn with sweat:
Thou, nestling, folding close and firm yet soft,
                companion better than talk, book, art,
(Thou hast, O Nature! elements! utterance to my
             heart beyond the rest—and this is of them,)
So sweet thy primitive taste to breathe within—thy
                 soothing fingers on my face and hands,
Thou, messenger-magical strange bringer to body and
                                  spirit of me,
(Distances balk'd—occult medicines penetrating me
                           from head to foot,)

I feel the sky, the prairies vast—I feel the mighty
                                        northern lakes,
I feel the ocean and the forest—and somehow I feel the
                                globe itself swift-swimming in space;
Thou blown from lips so loved, now gone—haply from
                                        endless store, God-sent,
(For thou art spiritual, Godly, most of all known to
                                        my sense,)
Minister to speak to me, here and now, what word has
                                never told, and cannot tell,
Art thou not universal concrete's distillation? Law's,
                        all Astronomy's last refinement?
Hast thou no soul? Can I not know, identify thee?

When I Heard the Learn'd Astronomer

When I heard the learn'd astronomer,
When the proofs, the figures were ranged in columns
                                        before me,
When I was shown the charts and diagrams, to add,
                                divide, and measure them,
When I sitting heard the astronomer where he
        lectured with much applause in the lecture-room,
How soon unaccountable I became tired and sick,
Till rising and gliding out I wander'd off by myself,
In the mystical moist night-air, and from time to time,
Look'd up in perfect silence at the stars.

To a Locomotive in Winter

Thee for my recitative,
Thee in the driving storm even as now, the snow,
                     the winter-day declining,
Thee in thy panoply, thy measur'd dual throbbing and
                     thy beat convulsive,
Thy black cylindric body, golden brass and silvery steel,
Thy ponderous side-bars, parallel and connecting
                 rods, gyrating, shuttling at thy sides,
Thy metrical, now swelling pant and roar,
                    now tapering in the distance,
Thy great protruding head-light fix'd in front,
Thy long, pale, floating vapor-pennants, tinged with
                     delicate purple,
The dense and murky clouds out-belching
                   from thy smokestack,
Thy knitted frame, thy springs and valves, the
                 tremulous twinkle of thy wheels,
Thy train of cars behind, obedient, merrily following,
Through gale or calm, now swift, now slack, yet
                   steadily careering;
Type of the modern—emblem of motion and power—
                   pulse of the continent,
For once come serve the Muse and merge in verse,
                   even as here I see thee,
With storm and buffeting gusts of wind and falling snow,

By day thy warning ringing bell to sound its notes,
By night thy silent signal lamps to swing.

Fierce-throated beauty!
Roll through my chant with all thy lawless music, thy
                                    swinging lamps at night,
Thy madly-whistled laughter, echoing, rumbling like
                                    an earthquake, rousing all,
Law of thyself complete, thine own track firmly holding,
(No sweetness debonair of tearful harp or glib piano
                                                    thine,)
Thy trills of shrieks by rocks and hills return'd,
Launch'd o'er the prairies wide, across the lakes,
To the free skies unpent and glad and strong.

Night on the Prairies

Night on the Prairies,
The supper is over, the fire on the ground burns low,
The wearied emigrants sleep, wrapt in their blankets;
I walk by myself—I stand and look at the stars, which
                    I think now I never realized before.

Now I absorb immortality and peace,
I admire death and test prepositions.

How plenteous! how spiritual! how resume!
The same old man and soul—the same old aspirations,
                                        and the same content.

I was thinking the day most splendid till I saw what
                            the not-day exhibited,
I was thinking this globe enough till there sprang out
            so noiseless around me myriads of other globes.

Now while the great thoughts of space and eternity fill
                    me I will measure myself by them,
And now touch'd with the lives of other globes arrived
                        as far along as those of the earth,
Or waiting to arrive, or pass'd on farther than those of
                            the earth,
I henceforth no more ignore them than I ignore my
                        own life,
Or the lives of the earth arrived as far as mine, or
                        waiting to arrive.
O I see now that life cannot exhibit all to me, as the
                        day cannot,
I see that I am to wait for what will be exhibited by
                                        death.

OF LIFE AND LOVE

Out of the Rolling Ocean the Crowd

Out of the rolling ocean the crowd came a drop
                     gently to me,
Whispering *I love you, before long I die,*
I have travel'd a long way merely to look on you to
                      touch you,
For I could not die till I once look'd on you,
For I fear'd I might afterward lose you.

Now we have met, we have look'd, we are safe,
Return in peace to the ocean my love,
I too am part of that ocean my love, we are not so
                   much separated,
Behold the great rondure, the cohesion of all,
                   how perfect!
But as for me, for you, the irresistible sea
                 is to separate us,
As for an hour carrying us diverse, yet cannot carry us
                 diverse forever;
Be not impatient—a little space—know you I salute
                 the air, the ocean and the land,
Every day at sundown for your dear sake my love.

I Saw in Louisiana a Live-Oak Growing

I saw in Louisiana a live-oak growing,
All alone stood it and the moss hung down
                              from the branches,
Without any companion it grew there uttering joyous
                              leaves of dark green,
And its look, rude, unbending, lusty, made me think
                              of myself,
But I wonder'd how it could utter joyous leaves stand-
    ing alone there without its friend near,
                              for I knew I could not,
And I broke off a twig with a certain number of leaves
                upon it, and twined around it a little moss,
And brought it away, and I have placed it in sight in
                              my room,
It is not needed to remind me as of my own
                              dear friends,
(For I believe lately I think of little else than of them,)
Yet it remains to me a curious token, it makes me think
                              of manly love;
For all that, and though the live-oak glistens there in
                Louisiana solitary in a wide flat space,
Uttering joyous leaves all its life without a friend a
                              lover near,
I know very well I could not.

One Hour To Madness and Joy

One hour to madness and joy! O furious! O confine
                                                me not!
(What is this that frees me so in storms?
What do my shouts amid lightnings and raging winds
                                                mean?)
O to drink the mystic deliria deeper than any other man!
O savage and tender achings! (I bequeath them to you
                                                my children,
I tell them to you, for reasons, O bridegroom and bride.)
O to be yielded to you whoever you are, and you to be
                                                yielded to me in defiance of the world!
O to return to Paradise! O bashful and feminine!
O to draw you to me, to plant on you for the first time
                                                the lips of a determin'd man.

O the puzzle, the thrice-tied knot, the deep and dark
                                                pool, all untied and illumin'd!
O to speed where there is space enough and air enough
                                                at last!
To be absolv'd from previous ties and conventions, I
                                                from mine and you from yours!
To find a new unthought-of nonchalance with the best
                                                of Nature!
To have the gag remov'd from one's mouth!
To have the feeling to-day or any day I am sufficient
                                                as I am.

O something unprov'd! something in a trance!
To escape utterly from others' anchors and holds!
To drive free! to love free! to dash reckless and dangerous!
To court destruction with taunts, with invitations!
To ascend, to leap to the heavens of the love indicated to me!
To rise thither with my inebriate soul!
To be lost if it must be so!
To feed the remainer of life with one hour of fulness
                                        and freedom!
With one brief hour of madness and joy.

A Noiseless Patient Spider

A noiseless patient spider,
I mark'd where on a little promontory it stood isolated,
Mark'd how to explore the vacant vast surrounding,
It launch'd forth filament, filament, filament, out of itself,
Ever unreeling them, ever tirelessly speeding them.

And you O my soul where you stand,
Surrounded, detached, in measureless oceans of space,
Ceaselessly musing, venturing, throwing, seeking the
                                        spheres to connect them,
Till the bridge you will need be form'd, till the ductile
                                        anchor hold,
Till the gossamer thread you fling catch somewhere,
                                        O my soul.

OF PARTING

When Lilacs Last in the Dooryard Bloom'd
[Written in honor of Abraham Lincoln]

1

When lilacs last in the dooryard bloom'd,
And the great star early droop'd in the western sky in
the night,
I mourned, and yet shall mourn with ever-returning
spring.

Ever-returning spring, trinity sure to me you bring,
Lilac blooming perennial and drooping star in the west,
And thought of him I love.

2

O powerful western fallen star!
O shades of night—O moody, tearful night!
O great star disappear'd—O the black murk that hides
the star!
O cruel hands that hold me powerless—O helpless soul
of me!
O harsh surrounding cloud that will not free my soul.

3

In the dooryard fronting an old farm-house near the
whitewash'd palings,
Stands the lilac-bush tall-growing with heart-shaped
leaves of rich green,
With many a pointed blossom rising delicate, with the
perfume strong I love,
With every leaf a miracle—and from this bush in the
dooryard,
With delicate-color'd blossoms and heart-shaped leaves
of rich green,
A sprig with its flower I break.

4

In the swamp in secluded recesses,
A shy and hidden bird is warbling a song.

Solitary the thrush,
The hermit withdrawn to himself, avoiding the
settlements,
Sings by himself a song.

Song of the bleeding throat,
Death's outlet song of life, (for well dear brother
I know,
If thou wast not granted to sing thou would'st
surely die.)

5

Over the breast of the spring, the land, amid cities,
Amid lanes and through old woods, where lately the
      violets peep'd from the ground, spotting the gray
            debris,
Amid the grass in the fields each side of the lanes,
            passing the endless grass,
Passing the yellow-spear'd wheat, every grain from its
      shroud in the dark-brown fields uprisen,
Passing the apple-tree blows of white and pink
            in the orchards,
Carrying a corpse to where it shall rest in the grave,
Night and day journeys a coffin.

6

Coffin that passes through lanes and streets,
Through day and night with the great cloud
            darkening the land,
With the pomp of the inloop'd flags with the cities
            draped in black,
With the show of the States themselves as
            of crape-veil'd women standing,
With processions long and winding and the flambeaus
            of the night,
With the countless torches lit, with the silent sea of
      faces and the unbared heads,

With the waiting depot, the thousand voices rising
strong and solemn,
With all the mournful voices of the dirges pour'd
around the coffin,
The dim-lit churches and the shuddering organs—
where amid these you journey,
With the tolling tolling bells' perpetual clang,
Here, coffin that slowly passes,
I give you my sprig of lilac.

7

(Nor for you, for one alone,
Blossoms and branches green to coffins all I bring,
For fresh as the morning, thus would I chant a song
for you O sane and sacred death.

All over bouquets of roses,
O death, I cover you over with roses and early lilies,
But mostly and now the lilac that blooms the first,
Copious I break, I break the sprigs from the bushes,
With loaded arms I come, pouring for you,
For you and the coffins all of you O death.)

8

O western orb sailing the heaven,
Now I know what you must have meant as a month
                                       since I walk'd,
As I walk'd in silence the transparent shadowy night,
As I saw you had something to tell, as you bent to me
                                       night after night,
As you droop'd from the sky low down, as if to my
           side, (while the other stars all look'd on;)
As we wander'd together the solemn night, (for some-
           thing, I know not what kept me from sleep;)
As the night advanced, and I saw on the rim of the
           west, ere you went, how full you were of woe;
As I stood on the rising ground in the breeze,
                          in the cold transparent night,
As my soul, in its trouble, dissatisfied, sank, as where
                                       you, sad orb,
Concluded, dropt in the night, and was gone.

9

Sing on, there in the swamp!
O singer bashful and tender! I hear your notes—I hear
                                       your call;
I hear—I come presently—I understand you;
But a moment I linger—for the lustrous star
                                 has detain'd me;
The star, my departing comrade, holds and detains me.

O how shall I warble myself for the dead one there I
loved?
And how shall I deck my song for the large sweet soul
that has gone?
And what shall my perfume be, for the grave
of him I love?

Sea-winds, blown from east and west,
Blown from the eastern sea, and blown from the
western sea, till there on the prairies meeting:
These, and with these, and the breath of my chant,
I perfume the grave of him I love. . . .

O Captain! My Captain!

O Captain! my Captain! our fearful trip is done,
The ship has weather'd every rack, the prize we
sought is won,
The port is near, the bells I hear, the people all
exulting,
While follow eyes the steady keel, the vessel grim and
daring;
But O heart! heart! heart!
O the bleeding drops of red,
Where on the deck my Captain lies,
Fallen cold and dead.

O Captain! my Captain! rise up and hear the bells;
Rise up—for you the flag is flung—for you the bugle
trills,
For you bouquets and ribbon'd wreaths—for you the
shores a-crowding,
For you they call, the swaying mass, their eager faces
turning;
Here Captain! dear father!
This arm beneath your head!
It is some dream that on the deck,
You've falled cold and dead.
My Captain does not answer, his lips are pale and still,
My father does not feel my arm, he has no pulse nor
will,
The ship is anchor'd safe and sound, its voyage closed
and done,
From fearful trip the victor ship comes in with
object won;
Exult O shores, and ring O bells!
But I with mournful tread,
Walk the deck my Captain lies,
Fallen cold and dead.

After the Supper and Talk

After the supper and talk—after the day is done,
As a friend from friends his final withdrawal
prolonging,
Good-bye and Good-bye with emotional lips repeating,
(So hard for his hand to release those hands—no more
will they meet,
No more for communion of sorrow and joy, of old and
young,
A far-stretching journey awaits him, to return
no more,)
Shunning, postponing severance—seeking to ward off
the last word ever so little,
E'en at the exit-door turning—charges superfluous
calling back—e'en as he descends the steps,
Something to eke out a minute additional—shadows
of nightfall deepening,
Farewells, messages lessening—dimmer the
forthgoer's visage and form,
Soon to be lost for aye in the darkness—loth, O so loth
to depart!
Garrulous to the very last.

PROSE THOUGHTS

Vast and Mystic Currents

My thoughts went floating on vast and mystic currents
as I sat today in solitude and half-shade by the creek—
returning mainly to two principal centers. One of my
cherished themes for a never-achieved poem has been
the two impetuses of man and the universe—in the
latter, creation's incessant unrest, exfoliation. (Dar-
win's evolution, I suppose.) Indeed, what is Nature
but change, in all its visible, and still more its invisible
processes? Or what is humanity in its faith, love, hero-
ism, poetry, even morals, but *emotion?*

Women in America

Democracy, in silence, biding its time, ponders its own
ideals, not of literature and art only—not of men only,
but of women. The idea of the women of America, (ex-
tricated from this daze, this fossil and unhealthy air
which hangs about the word *lady*) developed, raised
to become the robust equals, workers, and, it may be,
even practical and political deciders with the men—
greater than man, we may admit, through their divine

maternity, always their towering, emblematic attri-
bute—but great, at any rate, as man, in all departments; or, rather, capable of being so, soon as they
realize it, and can bring themselves to give up toys and
fictions, and launch forth, as men do, amid real, in-
dependent, stormy life.

The Chess Game of a Poem

The play of Imagination, with the sensuous objects of
Nature for symbols, and Faith—with Love and Pride
as the unseen impetus and moving-power of all, make
up the curious chess-game of a poem.

Common teachers or critics are always asking
"What does it mean?" Symphony of fine musician, or
sunset, or sea-waves rolling up the beach—what do
they mean? Undoubtedly in the most subtle-elusive
sense they mean something—as love does, and religion
does, and the best poems;—but who shall fathom and
define those meanings? (I do not intend this as a war-
rant for wildness and frantic escapades—but to justify
the soul's frequent joy in what cannot be defined to
the intellectual part, or to calculation.)

At its best, poetic lore is like what may be heard of
conversation in the dusk, from speakers far or hid, of
which we get only a few broken murmurs. What is not
gathered is far more—perhaps the main thing.

47

Glimpses of the Sublime

Curious as it may seem, it is in what are call'd the poorest, lowest characters you will sometimes, nay generally, find glints of the most sublime virtues, eligibilities, heroisms. Then it is doubtful whether the State is to be saved, either in the monotonous long run, or in tremendous special crises, by its good people only.

Abraham Lincoln

Abraham Lincoln's was really one of those characters, the best of which is the result of long trains of cause and effect—needing a certain spaciousness of time, and perhaps even remoteness, to properly enclose them—having unequal'd influence on the shaping of this Republic (and therefore the world) as to-day, and then far more important in the future. Thus the time has by no means yet come for a thorough measurement of him. Nevertheless, we who live in his era—who have seen him, and heard him, face to face, and are in the midst of, or just parting from, the strong and strange events which he and we have had to do with— can in some respects bear valuable, perhaps indispensable testimony concerning him. . . . Abraham Lincoln seems to me the grandest figure yet, on all the crowded canvas of the Nineteenth Century.

Absolute Balance

There is, apart from mere intellect, in the makeup of every superior human identity, (in its moral completeness, considered as *ensemble*, not for that moral alone, but for the whole being, including physique,) a wondrous something that realizes without argument, frequently without what is called education, (though I think it the goal and apex of all education deserving the name)—an intuition of the absolute balance, in time and space, of the whole of this multifarious, mad chaos of fraud, frivolity, hoggishness—this revel of fools, and incredible make-believe and general unsettledness, we call *the world*; a soul-sight of that divine clue and unseen thread which holds the whole congeries of things, all history and time, and all events, however trivial, however momentous, like a leashed dog in the hand of the hunter.

Beauty

All beauty comes from beautiful blood and a beautiful brain. If the greatnesses are in conjunction in a man or woman, it is enough—the fact will prevail through the universe; but the gaggery and gilt of a million years will not prevail.

The Weather

Whether the rains, the heat and cold, and what under-
lies them all, are affected with what affects man in
masses, and follow his play of passionate action,
strained stronger than usual, and on a larger scale
than usual—whether this, or no, it is certain that there
is now, and has been for twenty months or more, on
this American continent north, many a remarkable,
many an unprecedented expression of the subtle world
of air above us and around us.

There are since this Civil War, and the wide and
deep national agitation, strange analogies, different
combinations, a different sunlight, or absence of it;
different products even out of the ground. After every
great battle, a great storm. Even civic events the same.

On Saturday last a forenoon like whirling demons,
dark, with slanting rain, full of rage; and then the
afternoon, so calm, so bathed with flooding splendor
from heaven's most excellent sun, with atmosphere of
sweetness; so clear, it showed the stars, long, long before they were due. As President [Lincoln] came out
on the capitol portico, a curious little white cloud, the
only one in that part of the sky, appeared like a hover-
ing bird, right over him.

Poetry in Cities

The splendor, picturesqueness, and oceanic amplitude
and rush of these great cities, the unsurpassed situa-
tion, rivers and bay, sparkling sea-tides, costly and
lofty new buildings, facades of marble and iron, of
original grandeur and elegance of design, with the
masses of gay color, the preponderance of white and
blue, the flags flying, the endless ships, the tumultuous
streets . . . these, I say, and the like of these, completely
satisfy my senses of power, fullness, motion, and give
me, through such senses and appetites, and through
my aesthetic conscience, a continued exaltation and
absolute fulfillment.

Credo

Love the earth and sun and the animals, despise riches,
give alms to everyone that asks, stand up for the stupid
and crazy, devote your income and labor to others,
hate tyrants, argue not concerning God, have patience
and indulgence toward the people, take off your hat to
nothing known or unknown, or to any man or number
of men—go freely with uneducated persons, and with
the young, and with the mothers of families—re-
examine all you have been told in school or church or
in any book, and dismiss whatever insults your own

soul; and your very flesh shall be a great poem and have the richest fluency, not only in its words, but in the silent lines of its lips and face, and between the lashes of your eyes, and in every motion and joint of your body.

A Winter Day on the Beach

The attractions, fascinations there are in sea and shore! How one dwells on their simplicity, even vacuity! What is it in us, arous'd by those indirections and directions? That spread of waves and gray-white beach, salt, monotonous, senseless—such an entire absence of art, books, talk, elegance—so indescribably comforting, even this winter day—grim, yet so delicate-looking, so spiritual—striking emotional, impalpable depths, subtler than all the poems, paintings, music, I have ever read, seen, heard.

A Race of Singers

I say no land or people or circumstances ever existed so needing a race of singers and poems differing from all others, and rigidly their own, as the land and people and circumstances of our United States need such singers and poems today, and for the future.

On the Death of President Lincoln

April 16, 1865.—I find in my notes of the time, this passage on the death of Abraham Lincoln: He leaves for America's history and biography, so far, not only its most dramatic reminiscence—he leaves, in my opinion, the greatest, best, most characteristic, artistic, moral personality. Not but that he had faults, and showed them in the Presidency; but honesty, goodness, shrewdness, conscience, and (a new virtue, unknown to other lands, and hardly yet really known here, but the foundation and tie of all, as the future will grandly develop) *Unionism*, in its truest and amplest sense, formed the hard-pan of his character. These he sealed with his life.

The tragic splendor of his death, purging, illuminating all, throws round his form, his head, an aureole that will remain and will grow brighter through time, while history lives, and love of country lasts. By many has this Union been helped; but if one name, one man, must be picked out, he, most of all, is the conservator of it, to the future. He was assassinated—but the Union is not assassinated—*ca ira!* One falls, and another falls. The soldier drops, sinks like a wave—but the ranks of the ocean eternally press on. Death does its work, obliterates a hundred, a thousand—President, general, captain, private—but the Nation is immortal.

A Great Average

Our American superiority and vitality are in the bulk of our people, not in a gentry like the old world. The greatness of our army during the secession war, was in the rank and file, and so with the nation. Other lands have their vitality in a few, a class, but we have it in the bulk of the people. Our leading men are not of much account and never have been, but the average of the people is immense, beyond all history. Sometimes I think in all departments, literature and art included, that will be the way our superiority will exhibit itself. We will not have great individuals or great leaders, but a great average bulk, unprecedentedly great.

The Work of Man

I realize that not Nature alone is great in her fields of freedom and the open air, in her storms, the shows of night and day, the mountains, forests, sea—but in the artificial, the work of man too is equally great—in this profusion of teeming humanity—in these ingenuities, streets, goods, houses, ships—these hurrying, feverish, electric crowds of men, their complicated business genius . . . and all this mighty, many-threaded wealth and industry concentrated here.

Enjoying Nature

You must not know too much, or be too precise or scientific about birds and trees and flowers and watercraft; a certain free margin, and even vagueness—perhaps ignorance, credulity—helps your enjoyment of these things.

Locusts

Reedy monotones of locust, or sounds of katydid—I hear the latter at night, and the other both day and night. I thought the morning and evening warble of birds delightful; but I find I can listen to these strange insects with just as much pleasure. A single locust is now heard near noon from a tree two hundred feet off, as I write—a long whirring, continued, quite loud noise graded in distinct whirls, or swinging circles, increasing in strength and rapidity up to a certain point, and then a fluttering, quiet tapering fall. Each strain is continued from one to two minutes. The locust-song is very appropriate to the scene—gushes, has meaning, is masculine, is like some fine old wine, not sweet, but far better than sweet.

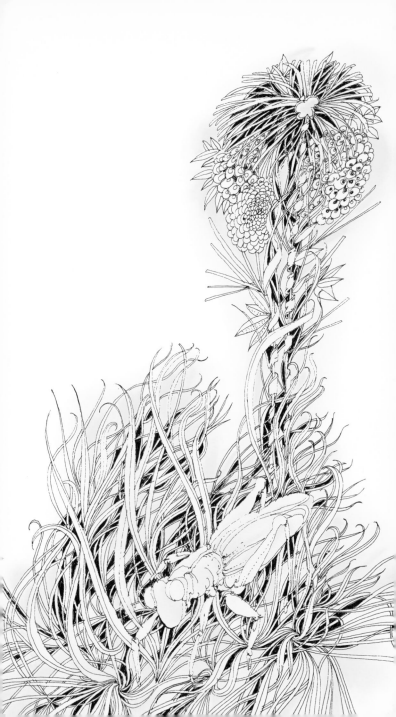

Language

Language, be it remember'd, is not an abstract con-
struction of the learn'd, or of dictionary-makers, but is
something arising out of the work, needs, ties, joys,
affections, tastes, of long generations of humanity, and
has its bases broad and low, close to the ground. Its
final decisions are made by the masses, people nearest
the concrete, having most to do with actual land and
sea. It impermeates all, the past as well as the present,
and is the grandest triumph of the human intellect.

The Artist in All Men

It is a beautiful truth that all men contain something
of the artist in them. . . . I think of few heroic actions,
which cannot be traced to the artistical impulse. He
who does great deeds, does them from his innate sensi-
tiveness to moral beauty. Such men are not merely
artists, they are also artistic material. Washington in
some great crisis, Lawrence on the bloody deck of the
Chesapeake, Mary Stuart at the block, Kossuth in cap-
tivity, and Mazzini in exile—all great rebels and in-
novators, exhibit the highest phases of the artist spirit.
The painter, the sculptor, the poet, express heroic
beauty better in description, but the others *are* heroic
beauty, the best beloved of art.

Nature in Procession

Nature marches in procession, in sections, like the corps of an army. All have done much for me, and still do. But for the last two days it has been the great wild bee, the humble-bee or "bumble," as the children call him. As I walk, or hobble, from the farmhouse down to the creek, I traverse the lane, fenced by old rails, with many splits, splinters, breaks, holes, &c., the choice habitat of those crooning, hairy insects. Up and down and by and between these rails, they swarm and dart and fly in countless myriads. As I wend slowly along, I am often accompanied with a moving cloud of them.

They play a leading part in my morning, midday or sunset rambles, and often dominate the landscape in a way I never before thought of—fill the long lane, not by scores or hundreds only, but by thousands. Large and vivacious and swift, with wonderful momentum and a loud swelling perpetual hum, varied now and then by something almost like a shriek, they dart to and fro, in rapid flashes, chasing each other, and (little things as they are), conveying to me a new and pronounced sense of strength, beauty, vitality and movement.

A Discovery of Old Age

Perhaps the best is always cumulative. One's eating and drinking one wants fresh, and for the nonce, right off, and have done with it—but I would not give a straw for that person or poem, or friend or city, or work of art, that was not more grateful the second time than the first—and more still the third. Nay, I do not believe any grandest eligibility ever comes forth at first. In my own experience (persons, poems, places, characters,) I discover the best hardly ever at first, (no absolute rule about it, however,) sometimes suddenly bursting forth, or stealthily opening to me, perhaps after years of unwitting familiarity, unappreciation, usage.